LEARN ABOUT VALUES

GENEROSITY

by Cynthia A. Klingel

Published in the United States of America by The Child's World®
1980 Lookout Drive • Mankato, MN 56003-1705 • 800-599-READ • www.childsworld.com

The Child's World®: Mary Berendes, Publishing Director; Katherine Stevenson, Editor
The Design Lab: Kathy Petelinsek, Art Director; Julia Goozen, Design and Page Production

Photo Credits: © David M. Budd Photography: 5, 9, 11; © Edward Bock/Corbis: cover, 15; © iStockphoto.com/Sharon Dominick: 13; © John Henley/Corbis: 17; © Pixland/Corbis: 19; © Randy Faris/Corbis: 21; © Richard Hutchings/Corbis: 7

Library of Congress Cataloging-in-Publication Data
Klingel, Cynthia Fitterer.
  Generosity / by Cynthia A. Klingel.
     p. cm. — (Learn about values)
  ISBN 978-1-59296-670-7 ISBN 1-59296-670-5 (library bound : alk. paper)
  1. Generosity—Juvenile literature. 2. Values—Juvenile literature. I. Title. II. Series.
  BJ1533.G4K55 2006
  179'.9—dc22   2006000972

CONTENTS

What Is Generosity?

Generosity is giving to others without expecting something in return. When you are generous, you want to help others. You are not thinking of yourself. You give because you want others to feel good.

Generosity is a way of being kind to others.

Generosity with Time

You have had a busy day at school. You have a lot to think about. You have a lot to do. Then you notice that your friend is sad. You are really busy! But you still take time to talk to him. You ask him if you can help. You show generosity by taking time to listen.

Sharing some time with people can really help them out.

Generosity with Food

You have brought cookies in your lunch. Your friend sits next to you. He does not have any cookies. The cookies you brought are your **favorite** kind. You would like to eat them all! But you know your friend likes them, too. You show generosity by sharing your cookies with him.

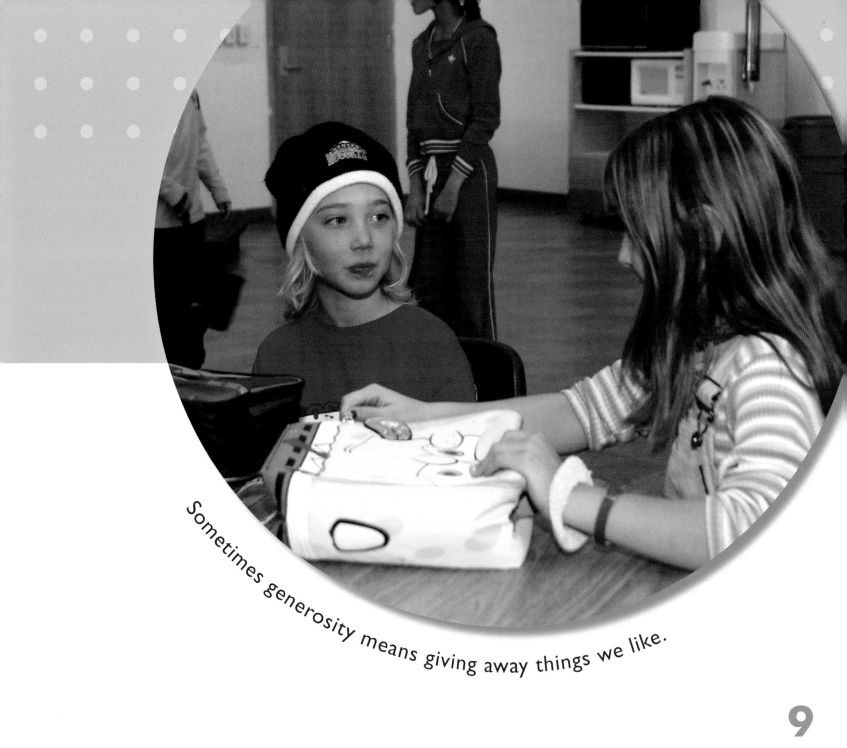

Sometimes generosity means giving away things we like.

Generosity with Your Things

You love to draw with markers. You have lots of markers in different colors. Other kids in your class do not have that many colors. You show generosity by sharing your markers. Now you can all have a better time drawing!

It feels good to share what you have.

Generosity **with Money**

You have been saving your money to buy a new toy. You cannot wait to get it! Then you learn in school about children in need. They do not have money for warm clothes. They do not have enough food. You would like to help them. You show generosity by **donating** some of your money.

You can show generosity by sharing money with people in need.

13

Generosity with Your Knowledge

Are you really good at something? Maybe you can sing. Maybe you know how to dance or draw. Or maybe you read really well. You can show generosity by sharing your knowledge. You can help somebody else learn these things. Teaching a younger kid can be fun! And it can make a big difference.

Helping your friends learn is a way to show generosity.

15

Generosity at Home

There are many ways to show generosity at home. You might not like your sister's favorite TV show. You can let your sister watch it anyway. Maybe feeding the dog is not your job. You can feed the dog anyway. Showing generosity is not just for friends and classmates. It is for family, too!

Being generous to your family is nice!

Generosity with Feelings

Maybe some people seem different from you. Maybe they do or say things you do not like. It might be easy to be mean to them. You could get upset. You could say, "I do not like you." But you show generosity instead. You try to understand their side. You give them a fair chance.

Generosity means not being too hard on people.

Generosity Makes a Difference!

Showing generosity means sharing with others. Sharing with people can really help them out. It makes their lives better. It makes your life better, too. How can you show generosity today?

Generosity makes the world a better place!

glossary

donating
Donating something is giving it away, often to people in need.

favorite
When you like something best, it is your favorite.

books

Hazen, Barbara Shook. *That Toad Is Mine!* (Growing Tree). New York: HarperFestival, 2001.

Napoli, Donna Jo. *How Hungry Are You?* New York: Atheneum, 2001.

Pearson, Mary. *Generous Me.* Chicago: Children's Press, 2002.

web sites

Visit our Web page for links about character education and values:
http://www.childsworld.com/links

Note to parents, teachers, and librarians:
We routinely check our Web links to make sure they're safe, active sites—so encourage your readers to check them out!

index

about the author

Cynthia A. Klingel is Director of Curriculum and Instruction for a school district in Minnesota. She enjoys reading, writing, gardening, traveling, and spending time with friends and family.